MW00928607

LET'S
see

Farm Machines

by Jennifer Blizin Gillis

Content Adviser: Susan Thompson, Agriculture Communications,
College of Agriculture, Iowa State University

Reading Adviser: Rosemary Palmer, Ph.D.,
Department of Literacy, College of Education,
Boise State University

Let's See Library
Compass Point Books
Minneapolis, Minnesota

The author would like to thank Lynn Mann of Manco Farms, Inc. in Pittsboro, N.C., for helping in the preparation of this book.

Compass Point Books
3109 West 50th Street, #115
Minneapolis, MN 55410

Visit Compass Point Books on the Internet at *www.compasspointbooks.com*
or e-mail your request to *custserv@compasspointbooks.com*

On the cover: A woman drives a tractor.

Photographs ©: Deere & Company, cover, 4, 6, 8, 10, 12; Corbis, 14; Richard Hamilton Smith, 16; The Image Finders/Michael Philip Manheim, 18; Unicorn Stock Photos/Eric R. Berndt, 20.

Creative Director: Terri Foley
Managing Editor: Catherine Neitge
Editors: Brenda Haugen and Christianne Jones
Photo Researcher: Marcie C. Spence
Designers: Melissa Kes and Jaime Martens
Educational Consultant: Diane Smolinski

Library of Congress Cataloging-in-Publication Data
Gillis, Jennifer Blizin, 1950-
 Farm machines / by Jennifer B. Gillis.
    p. cm. — (Let's see)
Includes bibliographical references (p.   ).
ISBN 0-7565-0672-7 (hardcover)
 1. Farm tractors—Juvenile literature. I. Title. II. Series.
S711.G55 2004
631.3'7—dc22   2003028296

Table of Contents

NOTE: In this book, words that are defined in the glossary
are in **bold** the first time they appear in the text.

Why Do Farmers Use Machines?

Farmers have always looked for easier, faster ways of doing work. Long ago, most farmwork was done by hand. Farmers needed many helpers. Farmers who did not have big families to help them had to hire workers. Now, machines make it possible for a few people to do the work of many.

The first farm machines were very simple. They were pushed or pulled by people or animals. As people learned more about steam- and gas-powered engines, they began making more powerful farm machines. Today, a farmer and one machine can do work that once took many people and many days to do.

◀ *A farmer lifts the hood on his tractor.*

What Are Tractors?

Tractors may be the most important farm machines. They pull or push **attachments** that do different jobs. Tractors also lift heavy loads and move them around the farm.

Tractors can weigh as much as 60,000 pounds (27,000 kilograms). That is as much as five or six adult elephants!

Farmers sit in tractor **cabs** that are like the insides of cars. The cabs have heat, air conditioning, and radios. Some tractors have **GPS receivers.** These help farmers know exactly where to plant rows of crops and apply **fertilizers** that help plants grow.

◀ *A tractor pulls an attachment called an ejector scraper, which helps level the land.*

Which Machines Get Fields Ready?

Plows and **discs** help farmers get the soil ready for each plant to take in water and **nutrients.** Crops need water and nutrients from the soil to grow.

Plows break up the soil and plants left over from old crops. Plows are made of sharp pieces of metal attached to a long bar. When the tractor plows a field, the sharp parts dig into the soil and break it up.

Discs have rows of round metal plates with very sharp edges. Farmers use discs to break up hard clumps of dirt or tough stalks of old plants.

◄ *A disc attached to the back of a tractor digs into the soil.*

Which Machines Are Used for Planting?

Most crops grow from seeds. Tractors pull attachments that put seeds into the ground. First one part opens very small holes in the ground and drops in seeds. Then another part covers the holes with soil. Farmers plant many rows of crops at one time. Farmers use these types of planters for bigger seeds, such as corn or cotton.

Another type of planter is a seed drill. It plants small seeds, such as wheat or oats. These kinds of crops grow much closer together in narrow rows. Sometimes the seeds are scattered to cover the entire field, like grass in a yard.

◄ *The planter attached to this tractor can plant corn and soybeans.*

Which Machines Feed and Weed Crops?

Farmers may put nutrients into the ground before planting crops. Tractors pull tanks of fertilizer. They also pull a bar that has sharp parts that cut into the soil. Then fertilizer runs from the tank into the soil. Crops may need more fertilizer as they grow. Then farmers drive tractors through the fields and add more near the plants' roots.

Weeds can harm crops by using the nutrients and water the crops need to grow. Farmers use cultivators to pull weeds out of the ground. Sometimes people ride on **rigs** through the fields and spray chemicals on the weeds to kill them.

◄ *This machine, called a cultivator, helps keep fields free from weeds.*

Which Machines Pick Crops?

Combines are big machines that **harvest** crops such as corn, other **grains,** and soybeans. The combines cut down many rows of plants, take the kernels or grains from the plants, put them into **hoppers** on the back of the combines, and dump the unwanted parts on the fields. When the hoppers are full, the kernels or grains are emptied from the combines into trucks or big wagons.

Farmers driving combines sit high up in the cabs. The cabs may have heat, air conditioning, and stereos. This helps make it easier for farmers to work long hours at harvest time.

◄ *A combine harvests corn.*

How Do Machines Help Store Crops?

Harvested crops must stay dry so they do not spoil. Machines help farmers quickly take crops from fields to storage places.

Baling machines form hay into square bales or huge rolls and tie them together. Rolled hay stays out in the field for animals to eat. Farmers store small bales of hay in buildings and barns.

Trucks or big wagons bring grain from the field to the farm. Grain is stored in buildings or **silos.** The grain is emptied out of the side or bottom of a truck or big wagon when a small door is opened. The grain falls into a machine called an auger that moves the grain into the silo.

◀ *A North Dakota farmer shovels grain toward an auger that carries it into a building.*

How Do Machines Help with Animals?

Milking machines milk cows. Workers put machines on the cows' **udders** to squeeze the milk out. The milk flows through tubes into a tank that keeps it cool.

Farmers use machines to help with laying hens. When the hens lay eggs, the eggs roll onto **conveyor belts.** The belts move the eggs to a room where they are washed, sorted by size, and packed.

Farmers also use machines to help feed pigs and cows. Farmers use feed grinders to mix together corn, soybeans, and other nutrients. Augers move the food from grinders to the feeders or **troughs.**

◄ *Machines milk cows.*

How Do Things Leave the Farm?

Trucks take crops that will be made into food away from farms. Some trucks are open, so you can see what is inside. Trucks also pull trailers carrying animals that will become meat for people to eat. Some animals may be in cages. Other animals are loose inside the trailers.

Milk leaves the farm in a **milk tanker.** The driver connects a hose from the tanker to a tank in the milking parlor that holds the milk. The milk is pumped into the tanker. Milk tankers keep the milk cool on the way to the dairy plant.

◄ *Corn is loaded from a combine into a truck.*

Glossary

attachments—parts or machines that must be hooked up to other machines in order to work

cabs—the enclosed spaces on combines and tractors where farmers sit to drive

conveyor belts—machines that can move things from one place to another

discs—farm machines with very sharp, round metal pieces that can chop up tough parts of old plants

fertilizers—materials that enrich the soil

GPS receivers—small computers that are part of the Global Positioning System of satellites

grains—seeds from plants such as corn, wheat, oats, or barley

harvest—to gather crops

hoppers—big boxes on the backs of combines

milk tanker—a truck with a special tank that keeps milk clean and cool

nutrients—the materials a living thing needs to live and grow

plows—machines with metal blades that break up and turn over dirt

rigs—machines people ride on so they can spray chemicals on weeds

silos—tall towers used to store grain

troughs—long, low containers used for feeding animals

udders—the baglike parts of cows that hang down near their back legs where milk is made

Did You Know?

• Potatoes grow underground, so they are harvested by digging machines. Workers known as potato harvesters pick up the newly dug potatoes and drop them into trucks.

• Machines shake nut trees to harvest the nuts. After the nuts fall to the ground, another machine vacuums up the nuts.

Want to Know More?

In the Library

Murphy, Andy. *Out and About at the Dairy Farm.* Minneapolis: Picture Window Books, 2003.

Rogers, Hal. *Combines.* Chanhassen, Minn.: Child's World, 2001.

Stille, Darlene. *Tractors.* Minneapolis: Compass Point Books, 2003.

Stone, Lynn M. *Farm Machinery.* Vero Beach, Fla.: Rourke Publishing, 2002.

On the Web

For more information on *farm machines,* use FactHound to track down Web sites related to this book.

1. Go to *www.facthound.com*
2. Type in a search word related to this book or this book ID: 0756506727.
3. Click on the *Fetch It* button.

Your trusty FactHound will fetch the best Web sites for you!

On the Road

Billings Farm and Museum
Route 12 and River Road
Woodstock, VT 05091-0489
802/457-2355
To see a working dairy farm

Queens County Farm Museum
73-50 Little Neck Parkway
Floral Park, NY 11004-1129
718/347-3276
To see farm machines, farm animals, and historic farm buildings

Index

About the Author

Jennifer Blizin Gillis writes poetry and nonfiction books for children. She lives on a former dairy farm in Pittsboro, North Carolina, with her husband, a dog, and a cat. She is more of a gardener than a farmer, but has lived on farms and in farming communities.